boyzone
go east!

"If anyone ever does a real book on us, we're bollixed." - Keith.

"What do you mean **if**?"- BP.

They invited me to go with them, to do a book, to travel with them through South East Asia and the Middle East and India.

I went for fun and came back with friendship. I liked all of the guys some of the time and most of the guys all of the time.

They were great hosts. I thank them.

Ronan, Steve, Shane, Keith and Mikey invited me into their world, half way round the world, for three and a half weeks.

It was a blast.

'Boyzone Go East!' is my way of telling the story, through Boyzone's own words in the Q & A, through the adventures we had on the way and mostly through the photographs of the madness, the beauty, the sadness and the joy.

I went to places I **didn't** know with people I got to know a little **and** love a lot.

Welcome.

First published in Great Britain in 1997 by Chameleon Books an imprint of Andre Deutsch Ltd, 106 Great Russell Street, London WC1B 3LJ

Andre Deutsch Ltd is a subsidiary of VCI plc.

The right of BP Fallon to be identified as the author of this work has been asserted by BP Fallon in accordance with the Copyright Design and Patents Act, 1988.

1098765432 1

Printed and bound in Great Britain by Butler and Tanner, Frome, Somerset.

A catalogue record for this book is available from the British Library

ISBN 0 233 99 3436

boyzone

go east!

photography and words by bp fallon
design and art direction by aba dublin

Ronan Patrick John Keating born on March 3rd 1977, at home on the Wilson Estate, Dublin, the only one in the family born at home.

Stephen Patrick David Gately, born St. Patrick's Day 1976.   **Shane** Eamon Mark Stephen Lynch, born July 3rd 1976.

Keith Peter Thomas Francis John Duffy, born October 1st 1974.   **Michael** Christopher Charles Graham, born August 15th 1972, Rotunda Hospital.

"All of the lads over the past four years have grown in different ways and all have matured an awful lot, for the better, definitely for the better - they've all become much wiser people." - Mikey

"The four of them I love very dearly. They have stood by me through any troubles or any faults and I couldn't ask for any better friends. They're four more brothers actually." - Steve

"Nobody in the band is perfect. I have had the best friends in each of them throughout the time in Boyzone so far. If you live with somebody so long you are going to have rows and arguments but I get on grand with all the boys - it's like growing up with brothers." - Keith.

BOYZONE 'A DIFFERENT BEAT' TOUR ITINERARY OF SOUTH EAST ASIA, MIDDLE EAST AND INDIA:

AUGUST: Wed 27th Fly from DUBLIN, IRELAND via LONDON, ENGLAND. Thur 28th Arrive Philippines, Cebu City. Fri 29th PHILIPPINES, CEBU CITY, CEBU COLISEUM. Sat 30th Fly to PHILIPPINES, MANILA, FOLK ARTS THEATRE. Sun 31st Fly to Taiwan, Taipei. SEPTEMBER: Mon 1st TAIWAN, TAIPEI, SUN YET SEN MEMORIAL HALL. Tue 2nd Fly to Korea, Seoul. Wed 3rd KOREA, SEOUL, '88 OLYMPIC TENNIS ARENA. Thur 4th Fly to Malaysia, Kuala Lumpur. Fri 5th Malaysia, Kuala Lumpur. Sat 6th MALAYSIA, KUALA LUMPUR, DERWAN WAWASAN. Sun 7th Fly to SINGAPORE, INDOOR STADIUM. Mon 8th Fly to Indonesia, Jakarta. Tue 9th INDONESIA, JAKARTA, BENGKEL NIGHT PARK. Wed 10th Fly to Indonesia, Surabaya. Thur 11th INDONESIA, SURABAYA, GO SKATE BUILDING. Fri 12th Fly to Indonesia, Bali. Sat 13th INDONESIA, BALI, TAMMAR FESTIVAL. Sun 14th Fly to Hong Kong. Mon 15th HONG KONG, COLISEUM. Tue 16th Fly to Bahrain, Manama. Wed 17th Bahrain, Manama. Thur 18th BAHRAIN, MANAMA, ON THE BEACH BESIDE LE ROYAL MERIDAN HOTEL. Fri 19th Fly to UNITED ARAB EMIRATES, DUBAI, AL NASR LEISURELAND then fly towards India. Sat 20th via Calcutta, arrive INDIA, BANGALORE, KANTEERAVA INDOOR STADIUM. Sun 21st India. Fly from Bangalore to BOMBAY for promotion and then fly towards home. Mon 22nd Via LONDON, ENGLAND arrive DUBLIN, IRELAND.

People are running around all over the place like washing powder that's been dropped into a bucket and stirred.

Melanie B from pop's new big bang The Spice Girls, crinkly electric hair an explosion on her head, shoots over and kisses the air beside a startled Mikey Boyzone. Robbie Williams, the former rebel from last year's teen gods Take That, is fighting the flab by sucking on a cardboard Coca Cola cup and chinwagging with Boyzone's Ronan and Steve. Louise Nurding, the ex-Eternal singer who sensibly trades under only her first name, stands to one side smiling nervously like a wind-up doll. She is just about to mime to her hit record 'Naked'.

The scene: London Arena, an antiseptic cavernous building in the reconstructed docklands, the site of the Smash Hits 1996 Poll Winners Party. Tomorrow afternoon 14,000 shrieking fans will be allowed entrance to this screamage holy of holies, this temple of teen.

But right now, rehearsals are in full swing on the stage that is suitably decorated like a funfair. Upstairs in the somewhat quieter Boyzone dressing room, Shane, a swathe of blonde hair dyed into his black quiff, and Keith, chipped front teeth and eyes like Bambi, are comparing their Porsches. Steve, childlike with an air of vulnerability, sits on the leather sofa whispering into his mobile, looking up and smiling shyly. Mikey, shaven-headed and groovy dark moody shades, sits beside Steve and gazes at the floor. Ronan, black leather coat, golden blonde hair and the most mischievous eyes in pop, paces around the room tearing open letters from fans, nervous energy in full flow, vibing up the rest of the band.

"What time is it?" Ronan says several times, looking at his watch.

"Time to sit down and relax" says Shane.

Steve comes off the phone and rips the wrapping from a Walt Disney Mickey Mouse doll which he waves at Keith.

"No time like a present" says Keith.

Mikey gazes at the ground...

Boyzone were formed in Dublin in November 1993. The first single by Ronan, Steve, Shane, Keith and Mikey, 'Working My Way Back To You', was released in Ireland in March 1994. In Britain, their first single was released in November 1994: 'Love Me For A Reason' entered the charts at No. 10 and climbed to No. 2 for Christmas. Candyfloss pop gobbled up by the hungry new converts.

On stage next afternoon and Lily Savage the drag queen with spindly legs and a wig like candyfloss presents Ronan in his leather coat with three awards: Best Haircut, Best Dressed Person. And Most Fanciable Person, where Ronan tops the poll ahead of Prince William who comes in fifth. Ronan, an easy smile that creases his cheeks just so, a warm twinkle shining naturally from his luggage eyes... this prince of pop, he's a natural. If children had the vote, this man would be Prime Minister. This week, anyway.

The cream of teen are on this Smash Hits show: Boyzone, Spice Girls, Peter Andre, Eternal, Louise, East 17 and Gabrielle, even Michael Jackson's nephews 3T. And when guitar groups like The Manic Street Preachers and Cast appear they look most odd because they don't even have dancers with them.

Now Boyzone are miming 'Words', having been presented with three more awards: Best International Group, Best Single and Best Album. The decibel level, 14,000 tonsils again displayed in their owners' baby-faced mouths, would drown out Concorde and tumble the walls of Babylon. It's the sound of seagulls at feeding time.

Back in the dressing-room Ronan, who hasn't eaten all day, suddenly feels faint and passes out.

Next day and the "Ronan Collapses" story screams from the front pages of the British tabloids, ahead of Mother Teresa fighting a heart, lung and kidney problem, a huge volcanic eruption in Zaire and Cardinal Hume meeting Prime Minister John Major with a cease-fire bid.

"I just needed a bit of sleep," says Ronan brightly. Needed? It's six o'clock in the morning now and we're already at GMTV with Boyzone about to be interviewed live in half an hour. Needed? God. Keith's been out all night, carousing at Groucho's club where, he tells you, Noel Gallagher was in attendance. Keith manages to look remarkably human.

Outside Boyzone's hotels, there are girls waiting. Outside the MTV studios, there are girls waiting. Outside the Noel Edmonds Breakfast Show at the BBC in White City, there are girls waiting. Outside Capital Radio, there are girls waiting. At the airport, there are girls waiting. Their information - some magic 20th Century bush telegraph. These fans, they always know where the Boyz are. Always.

Not a bad beginning. Since then Boyzone's two albums entered the British charts at No.1. Boyzone's last two singles 'Words' and 'A Different Beat' were No.1 records too. There has never been a pop group come out of Ireland like Boyzone. Last year in screamland it was Take That. The Spice Girls are knocking loudly, very loudly. But right now in this split second of teen scene scream time, Boyzone not only fly the flag – their picture is on it. And in the teen magazines and the newspapers and the gossip columns and on school books and in the dreams of effervescent young fans all over the world.

And what about the vibe that Boyzone are all squeaky clean. "We never said that we don't drink, that we don't smoke," says Shane, he of the split eyebrow and chains of gold. He looks intense and friendly at the same time. "We admit that we get drunk now and again. We're normal."

Another day and Shane and Steve open their suitcases and out falls white powdery stuff in bulging transparent plastic bags, the size of small pillows. The bags, they're filled with white stuff. There sure is a lot of white stuff in there. It's plastic snow, scammed from the floor manager at the TV programme The CITV Awards. There, they perform in the dome created by a huge snowman's tummy. There, there are Christmas trees and yup, plastic snow. There, they are competing with Oasis and Spice Girls and, gosh, Ant and Dec, for Best Group. And there, of course, Boyzone win.

The fans are so enchanting, little children from Central Casting in a Benetton ad. No, not literally, but that's the vibe. They're quiet and awed and easily shoved about by a technician, these kids, gorgeous, cute and mute. Their eyes marvel up at Boyzone miming, all of Boyzone stretching out their right arms at the same time. Then these mini-sized fans - we're talking 7, 8, maybe 9 years old - are steered away by someone like they were shepherding geese.

At The CITV Awards, the studio is quietened as the camera people prepare for their next positions. Presenter Danni Minogue twitches and preens. And, hidden out of sight, Boyzone prepare for their next entrance. They're all up there in this life-sized helter-skelter tower, hidden from view. In a minute they'll be sliding down onto the fake plastic snow and bumping into each other and scrambling to their feet and Shane will fall down in the confusion, just like people do in real life. But until this auspicious moment, they're invisible.

You can't see 'em as they wait high up inside the helter-skelter but you guess that somehow none of them is even talking on his mobile phone right now. It's just these five genuinely charming guys, these young friends who work together. There's a bond there, a bond that will always exist one way or another but a bond that will inevitably change. Right now they're as equal as they'll ever be. That'll change too.

The magic of pop is the magic of the moment, some tingle in time that multiplies, a gigantic emotional snowball of excitement and warmth, shared laughter and quieter dreams.

Boyzone pop out of the chute into the plastic snow, five famous pop stars, laughing.

Everywhere they go, this gang of Ronan, Steve, Shane, Keith and Mikey, the five lads from the Northside of Dublin, there are girls with photos to be signed, pictures to be taken, tears of joy to be seen.

It's like some miraculous blessing gone out of control.

Is all this a fantasy for the fans then? "On the fans behalf, yes," says Shane. "We wouldn't date a fan because what they see is on a big screen and not ourselves."

In the middle of all this camaraderie that you guys share, in the middle of all this madness, does it get lonely? "Very much", admits Ronan. "The loneliness of a hotel room is hard, sometimes, just waiting for the next day to turn around, not being able to sleep 'cos you've a million things in your head".

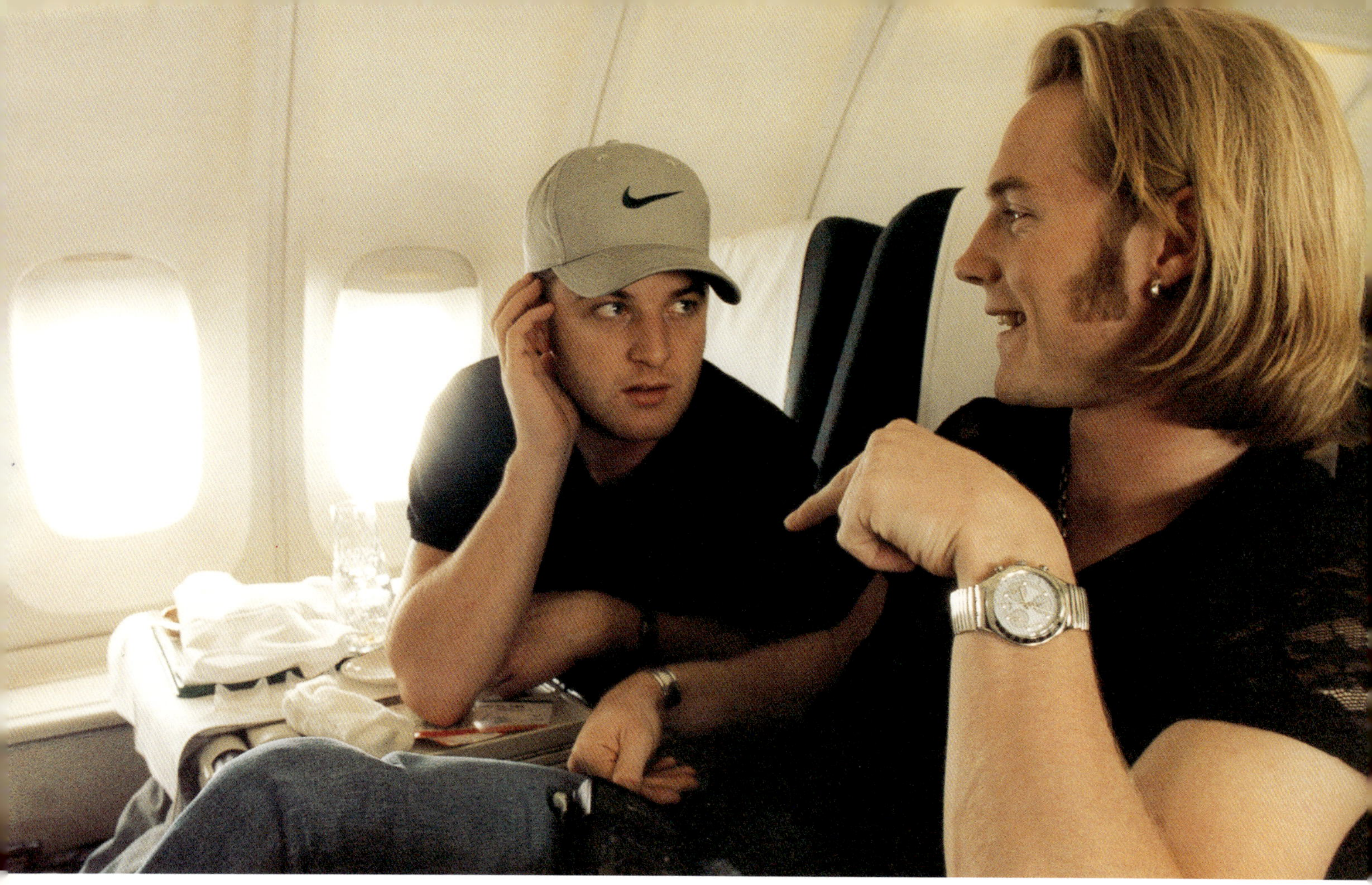

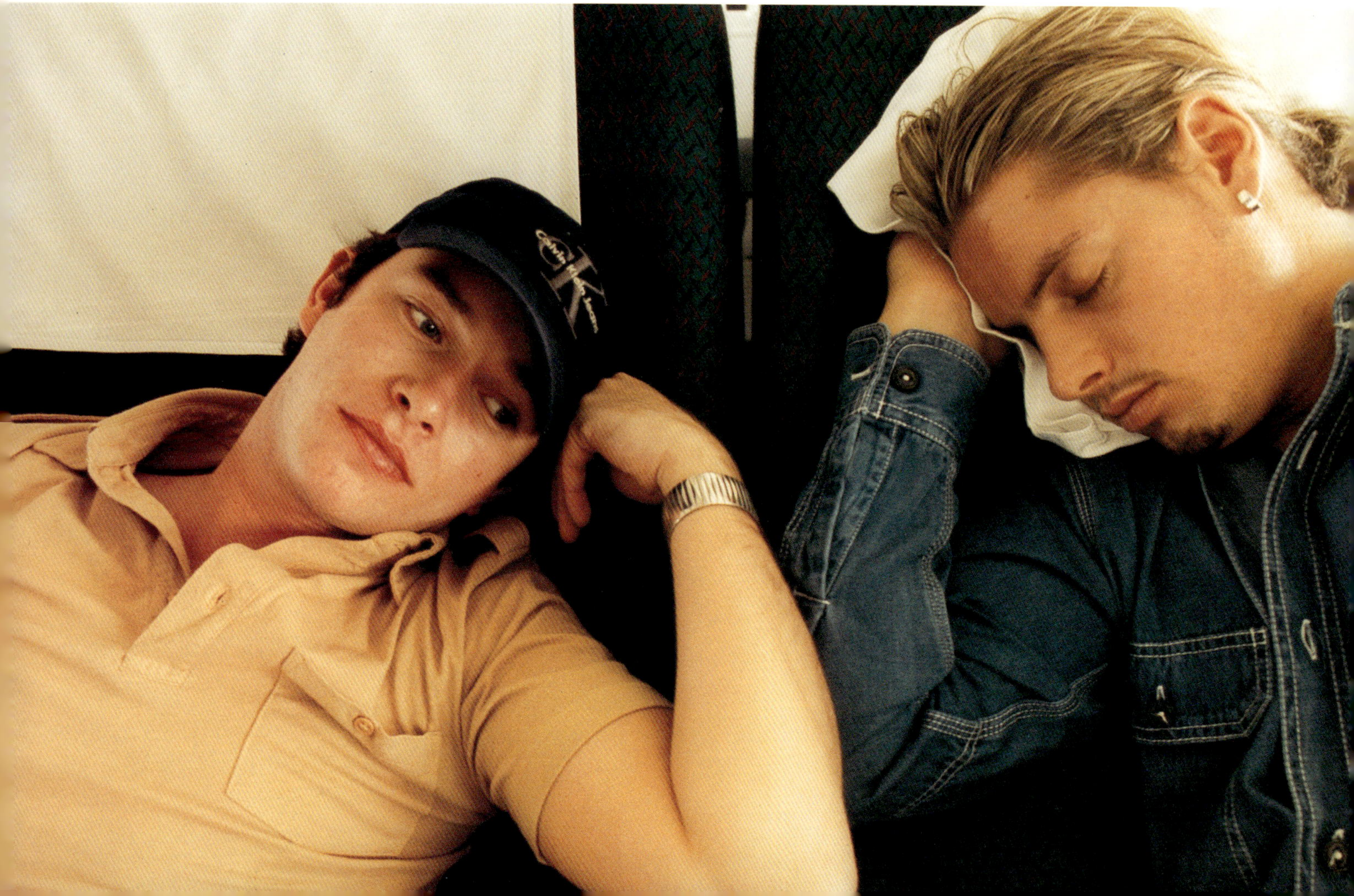

Boyzone work harder than any other group I've met. They work bloody hard. Here's a random day, Hong Kong on Monday September 15th 1997, the day of their concert:

12.00 - 12.35	Press conference & photo call at hotel (approx 40 people)
12.35 -12.50	Change clothes for photo session
12.50 - 1.35	Photo session for Young Generation Magazine cover (Request to change clothes for two shootings)
1.40 - 2.00	TV interview - ATV Saturday Music Video Express
2.00 - 2.15	TV interview - Cable YMC
2.15 - 2.30	TV interview - TVB Saturday Music Programme
2.30 -2.45	Meet and Greet with 10 competition winners (East Touch Magazine will take photos)
2.45 - 3.00	Radio interview - FM Select (Ronan & Mikey)
2.45 - 3.00	Radio interview - Hit Radio (Steve & Shane & Keith)
3.00 - 3.15	Radio interview - RTHK Radio 2 (Ronan & Mikey)
3.00 - 3.15	Press interview - East Touch (Steve & Shane & Keith)
3.15 - 3.25	Break
3.25 - 3.30	Drive to HMV
3.30 - 3.40	Singing session at HMV
4.30	Drive to venue for sound check

Then they do a show at the Hong Kong Coliseum.
Then they go to an aftershow party at Hot Gossip disco.

They can be found in the lobby of The Hong Kong Hotel at 6.30 in the morning, rather battered and the worst for wear. Next day they're up bright and early - well, some of them bright - to be interviewed on TV some more, before flying back all the way across India to Bahrain.

Photo by Barry Knight

Ronan: No, far from it. Never ever consider myself a sexy person. Couldn't be sexy if I tried!

BP: Who is sexy?

Ronan: Michelle Pfeiffer was sexy in that cat suit in 'Batman'. Anyone on the street can be sexy, it's how they walk, how they dress, how their eyes catch you, it's a presence about someone, sex.

Steve: Sexy as in sexy looking? Definitely not! I don't class myself as a good looking person and anyone could be doing the same thing I am if they wanted to – I just think that I got chosen.

Shane: I'll explain it in a female way. If I saw a woman in a pair of cowboy boots standing with a bra and knickers on, I would say that is sexy. If a woman was just really beautiful, dressed very elegant, I wouldn't say it's sexy but classy and I would more say that's what I am. I'm not a sexy person, I'm just a pretty cool bloke. I've got good style and I know people know I've a good style. I give out a good aura of 'I'm here and I'm pretty large'!

Mikey: I don't know if I am sexy. Sometimes maybe I am, once in a blue moon. Maybe because of a strength, of an exterior, the way I act, some women may find it attractive about me. They like the kind of, I won't say male dominance thing, but the male thing, a strength that they see within you as a person and mentally being strong. I think that's what they see as sexy.

Keith: Opinions vary. To some girls I might be sexy, to other girls I might be revolting. I don't feel sexy. My interpretation of sexy is a girl in a mini skirt but I don't think I'm sexy at all – I look stupid in a mini-skirt!

Shane: Stephen is just a little kid that's trying, in a good sense, to be a man. I'm not saying he's immature but he is out in a big bad world! He loves the attention and loves to think that people are shouting and screaming for him and he thrives on that, but he's not a leader. He's a very close friend of mine. I tell Stephen my deepest, darkest thoughts - we're very close.

Ronan: Steo is very sensitive. He's not the youngest but we all see him as being the youngest member of the band and we all take care of him. He's a very caring person, very loving, a good man.

Mikey: Stephen used to be a very shy, insecure and very hard to approach person. Now he's become very strong, very dominant in his opinions and his ways and a lot more friendly. He's a good guy, he has a good heart but he doesn't like anybody messing with him. I'm more of a friend with Stephen now than I ever have been.

Keith: Stephen is very deep, the deepest of the lot of us. It took me four years to get to know Stephen and I'm pretty much there now. He carries everything around on his shoulders, never forgets a thing. When he gets down he takes it out on the people closest to him and he won't speak to them for days. But he needs a hug, needs to be loved, looked after, needs support, needs security. He's lucky to have softies in the group around him because we've always looked after him. He's a little bollix at times with a vicious side to him but it's just because he is so soft that that's his aggression. The girls picture him as a real little cutie, soft nice boy and he is, but he has got another side to him that they don't know. But everybody's human! He's a good mate.

" 5 X 5　shane "

Ronan: Shanno is a very cool, calm, collected guy, likes to know what's going on, likes to be professional, has a good time, enjoys himself, goes to bed at night! A good man.

Mikey: Shane is solemn, sees things in his way, in his world. His shyness is probably misunderstood for ignorance sometimes which is wrong 'cos I know the guy from close up. He's a good guy, a friendly kind of fellow.

Steve: Shane is like my big brother - he looks after me and I'm very close to him. At times we argue but he's a great chap with a great sense of strength. If I'm in need of a hug he's the person to hug me, he's always concerned about me. Lovely person, nothing gets him down. I hope to live many more years having him as one of my best friends.

Keith: It's a difficult one really. I have to be diplomatic. Shane's a nice guy up front, but thinks he knows it all. Been a good mate, been a good enemy as well, at times. In general we get on well, we work together well. If the band ever finishes we won't be the best mates in the world. He has the perfect idea of himself in his head but he's not a perfect person – he's one of these people that can never ever admit he's wrong and can never apologise. He's a really good friend, a good friend to me and everyone in the band. Good image, very polite, nice guy, happy go lucky, doesn't want much out of life, he'd be happy with what he has now. Cool, very cool bloke.

" 5 X 5   mikey "

Steve: Mikey's intelligent, friendly, a good geezer. When he knows that you're really upset he is very concerned. He can be very funny at times.

Shane: At times we all have our moments of being on the edge but in general Mikey tells us boys nothing. Very close to his family and brothers-in-law and that kind of lark but as for the band, it's just music to him and nothing to do with his private life. Nice chap, I get on very well with Mikey - don't know on a scale of 1-10 how close mates we would be, but we're not that close, we just work together.

Keith: I have a fantastic friend in Mikey, we're very very alike. Unfortunately he has a lot of hang-ups about himself but he's his own worst enemy. We're both bad, both have bad sides to us, but it's a very fine line between love and hate. I think he feels his age a bit more than the rest of us now but he has a lot of talent. We've had our differences in the past but at the end of the day if anyone was to look crooked at him or hurt him in any way I would be very protective over him, I'd definitely help him out. He's a good mate and friend, a nice bloke.

Ronan: Mikey's the oldest, he drifts. Lot of stuff on Mick's mind, doesn't really talk to everybody, he spends a lot of time on his own. Really strong headed person though, a good man.

" 5 X 5   keith "

Mikey: Keith, he's big, he's loud, he's proud and he's a loving kind of guy. He's fun to be with, he's strong but there's a child there too that needs taking care of.

Ronan: Keith is a very carefree young man, likes to enjoy himself, have a good time. Good friend, always game for a laugh, always having a good time. Sensitive, very sensitive. Good man.

Shane: We were very close at one stage but we're very chalk and cheese. I disagree with nearly everything he says and vice versa. It's bitchiness, I think. But he's a really nice bloke, his heart is in the right place, he tries to please everybody. He's very easily led and I don't know if that's a downfall or not, or if that makes him happy. Nice guy.

Steve: If I'm ever in need of a laugh Keith is always there. If I'm scared, Keith's there. He's got a big heart, he's very funny, he makes me laugh.

Steve: Soul! A very good soul, not a bad bone in his body. He's a very, very dear friend and I feel so close to him. He understands me, I understand him and we've got a lot in common. He'll go a long way.

Shane: Ro is a good mate of mine and we've been through a lot together. He is a complete star and will always be in the music business. A star, a genuine bloke, no bullshit about him. He is quite soft but he does try hard to be hard.

Keith: I'd probably be closest to Ronan at the moment than I have been for the last while. Ronan is an absolute gentleman with a total respect for his elders that he's never lost. He cares about other people and not hurting them. If someone really pisses him off he has a great way about him, rising above the shit and still being polite. I have never ever seen anyone like him - people can put him down to his face in a really horrible way and he is still able to rise above it and be polite. It's such an art to be able to do that. He never gets riled - you get upset before you get a rise out of him. A lot of times though he wipes the dirt under the carpet just to be friends, when he should let it rip. It doesn't clear the air when you wipe it under the carpet. Sometimes he tells people what they want to hear. He's a mad bastard at times as well, a head-banger, just as bad as me! Still, I have the utmost respect for him and I think we will always be mates for as long as we're alive.

Mikey: Ronan, a young man, very very talented. I don't know if cunning would be the right word to use – he's sensible, his eyes are open, he knows what to do with himself. He knows what the best thing for himself is and he exploits himself in the best possible manner. But because he is such a young guy sometimes I would worry for him – he is so young to be so advanced for his age and I don't know if one day he may turn around and wonder where his youth has gone.

Bali: Sunday September 14th 1997

We go to the ancient Luhur Uluwatu temple, where the band dress in traditional Balinese costume, sarongs and all. While you're taking their picture a rascally monkey leaps from the wall and grabs the shades off your head. The monkey – he tries them on but luckily they don't fit. The monkey – he swops your shades for two bananas....

Then we fly to Hong Kong.

boyzone was shane's idea

"When I was 16 I knew I would be very successful in life but I didn't know it would be the music business. I was watching a TV show called 'Smash Hits'. I'm a fan of Will Smith and he was hosting that year. I was watchin' various bands and I thought 'I could do that, that's what I want to do'. I was 17, a mechanic at the time, didn't know if I could still sing. I was in a choir once! I got the name of Louis Walsh, called him up, asked to meet him, sat down and talked to him and said 'The next time Ireland has a pop group are you interested in managing it?' He said 'Yeah, great, wonderful, let's do it!' He didn't know nothin' about me, whether I could sing. I knew the lads through various different things - Mikey through college, Stephen through dancing. Ronan and Stephen had been mates and Keith I knew basically all my life. I knew Steo liked to sing and he was a good performer, disco dancing and stuff. Keith was a good looking chap, I didn't know if he could sing or dance but he had an image that would suit a pop star life. Mikey, I knew he was very influenced by music and he was in bands.

So I asked the boys to...well, to a certain extent there was an audition but there wasn't. We knew what the band was going to be but if we were going to have the best of the best in Ireland why not see what the other talent was all about? That's why we held auditions, but there was no one as good as us five so we kept it to us five. To be honest, in the beginning there were a couple of different people in the band but when we knew they didn't fit, we changed it to what it is right now and that's how it's been ever since.

We sang the George Michael song 'Careless Whisper', that's what we were told to do. Some people came in and did their own thing and played guitars. Some were hilarious, I killed myself laughin'. Luckily enough I didn't have to audition. As I said, Louis Walsh knew nothing about me, didn't even know if I could sing, but I just was in and that was it - one of those strange things in life.

The name Boyzone? It has brought us this far but I think every band hates their name and goes 'Why did we call ourselves that?' four years down the road. It was good at the time and it still is a good name as it's easy to remember, plain and simple - a lot of people world-wide now know that name so I can't knock it."

Louis Walsh is the dreamer and the warm-hearted schemer. U2 manager Paul McGuinness is a fan. Paul will tell you how Louis always had money in his pocket, long before managing Johnny Logan and Linda Martin and the Eurovision boogaloo. Paul himself was just starting out as a manager, managing this forgotten group called Spud and Paul. He kept asking Louis for some phone numbers and Louis kept saying "Yes, I'll get them for you." But he never did. So Paul gave Louis a hundred quid for these numbers and started ringing around, trying to get bookings for Spud. Everywhere Paul rang the answer was "Louis Walsh does all my bookings."

RONAN ON BOYZONE MANAGER LOUIS WALSH

"He's a character - he's a gas, man, a carefree person who loves music. He lives by his music, biggest record collection I've ever seen in my life. Knows every song, everyone that sung it, everyone that writes them. Lovely man, big heart, lot of time for him. Me and him have been very close for many years and will be for many more. Wonderful, wonderful person. He gave me the chance to be where I am today. I will never forget that, never, no way."

the bp boyzone q & a

* The BP Bz Q & A was conducted in Bangalore and Bombay, with each member responding without knowing what the others had answered.

WHAT'S IN YOUR POCKETS?

Steve: At the moment just a key for this hotel here, the Taj Mahal in Bombay. It's an interesting place, vibey, a bit mad. It's great but it's too dangerous to go out and do anything, more for the safety of the people than ourselves. There's a lot of girls out there 'cos things like this don't really happen that much in India. I'd say they'd just grab you to pieces...

Shane: My phone, room key, wallet and coins that I collect for my sister. She collects different kind of notes and coins so I have a pocket full of coins.

Keith: Absolutely nothing, a lighter that's all – just one I robbed off someone last night.

Mikey: A tape of Boyzone that I just received, it's the 'Different Beat' album, a special tour edition with five extra tracks on it. I've my room key from the Taj Mahal Hotel in Bombay, and a box of matches and my phone – that's my link to the rest of the world. The matches are from the Sheraton Towers which is in Bangalore in India.

Ronan: A pocket full of dreams...

WHEN DID YOU LAST CRY AND WHY?

Ronan: Last time I cried? Me mam, she got cancer a year and a half ago and she got the all clear three weeks ago. It was fantastic, thank God.

Steve: I shed a tear for Lady Di, Princess Diana's death. It's tragic. She was such a lovely person, an icon for people of the '90s, for teenagers of the '90s. When I was going to sing for her at the Disney premiere, even before anything happened her, I wanted to meet her and I was going to say, "You are such a great person, how do you cope with it, fair play to you". The admiration I had for her...

Keith: I had a tear in my eye on this tour. I was a bit down 'cos I was missing me son Jordan and me bird Lisa.

Mikey: (pause) I don't know, I can't remember. I find it very hard to show deep emotion. I just don't cry. It's not because I don't want to, I would like to. There's an awful lot inside me I would like to let out. Crying is a natural release valve for all the stress and shit in your life and if you have a good cry it can make you stronger. But because I can't cry it can make life tough.

Shane: Couldn't tell you B, it's been that long ago.
BP: Do you bottle stuff up emotionally?
Shane: No, I'm very happy the way I am, I don't need to cry.

Surabaya, Indonesia, Thursday 11th September, 1997.

You go with Mikey to Jalan Ampel Suci, the bazaar in the Arab quarter of Surabaya. Everyone stares, especially the kids who begin following him through the stalls until an almost-shy posse of youngsters fans out behind him, looking at each other and looking up at this man in the black kopiah Arab hat.

Someone appears with an Arabic newspaper and points to it. On the front cover is a colour photograph and an article on Boyzone.

manila, the philippines

Saturday 30th August, 1997. In Manila we're staying in this palatial hotel - grandly called
The Manila Hotel - that seems to be some warped testament to the richness
and opulence of the Marcos regime, when Ferdinand and Imelda, she of the
thousands of pairs of shoes, bloodsucked the country dry and lived in splendour.

It's the afternoon. Chandeliers dangle loudly. A string quartet plays soothing
rhapsodies. Ronan walks through the enormous entrance hall, cowboy hat
and denim. Girls scream. Flash cameras flash. Paper and pen wave in the
air. Startled matrons with blue hair and diamante studded glasses look
askance, then curious, then beam in recognition. "Aah yes,
Boyzone," they're going, all in affectionate agreement. The eldest
of these women, who looks about 97, stamps her cane on the
floor and says to her pal "Is that one Steve?".

live

The Boyzone concerts are wild. The gigs are crazy. From the opening chant of
"Forever!" from Ronan, Steve, Shane, Keith and Mikey, the audience goes ape.
They've been building up to this, sparked up with banners and little
cameras and hearts that are bursting.

Boyzone sing, Boyzone dance. Sometimes they're not the most
brilliant band in the world, but they have charm, they have
honesty. There's no bulsh about Boyzone, no pretension.

Screaming and fainting and crying and laughing have
always been part of pop, from the young Frank Sinatra
and his adoring bobby-soxers, to John, Paul, George
and Ringo and the Beatlemania of their fans, to Marc
Bolan and his joyful T. Rextasy.

Boyzone's backing group of Tim, Paul,
Richie and Guy, they pump it up, Guy's
drums pounding. Boyzone ignite their
hits, songs like 'Father and Son', 'A
Different Beat', 'I'll Be There', 'Words',
their Motown medley that they first did
on The MTV Awards. And then there's
'Isn't It A Wonder', their song of
openness, and rejoicing, of being one.
"Isn't it a wonder, on the crossroads of
my life..." **Fine** song.

And all the time Ronan, Steve, Shane,
Keith and Mikey are doing all these
movements, little dance routines, moving
their arms and their legs about in
patterns, doing this, doing that.

"I don't know how you remember all those
movements," you remark one night.

"Neither do I," says Ronan.

ARE YOU SURPRISED BY YOUR SUCCESS?

Mikey: No. I always knew from day one it was headed to where it was headed. I knew it was going to be a phenomenon. The only thing I was unsure of on a personal level was, was it what I wanted to do, was it me? But I have had to put that aside and concentrate on the job. I wouldn't complain about it, it has been a great experience, taught me an awful lot of things, brought me on as a person in leaps and bounds, made me a wiser man. Travelled the world, met many people, the experience, the opportunity is second to none. You can never knock something like this. Every single person in the world dreams of this kind of thing. It's a very pressured business, it's a fickle business but when we are away from the madding crowd and it's the five of us we can have a good laugh.

Ronan: Yeah. I always had hopes and dreams to be successful, but never as successful as we are and it's fantastic. Love it, surprised is an understatement.

Steve: Very glad of our success, very, very happy with the success. We have worked very hard for four years. I don't think people realise how hard we work, people just don't. People just see the glam and the glitz, the limousines, the cars. They don't see the background work. I remember one week we were up every morning at 4 to go on location to film 'The Big Breakfast in winter'. Just glad we have worked for what we got...

Shane: No, not me personally, I'm not. I always knew I would be rich and famous, always knew. From the time I was 16, and any of me mates will tell you that, I says "Before I'm 21 I'll own a Porsche". I was 19 when I first bought my Porsche. I always had my goals set very very high in life, didn't know how I was going to do it and I had nothing planned. But I always knew I would go a long way.

Keith: Absolutely, blown away by it, totally. I know that we're good performers. After a long time doing something you are bound to be good at it, and we are good at it now, good entertainers. We are not the best dancers, best singers in the world but we are entertainers, good personalities on stage, good performers, professional. We make people happy. I don't think anyone ever left a Boyzone concert disappointed...

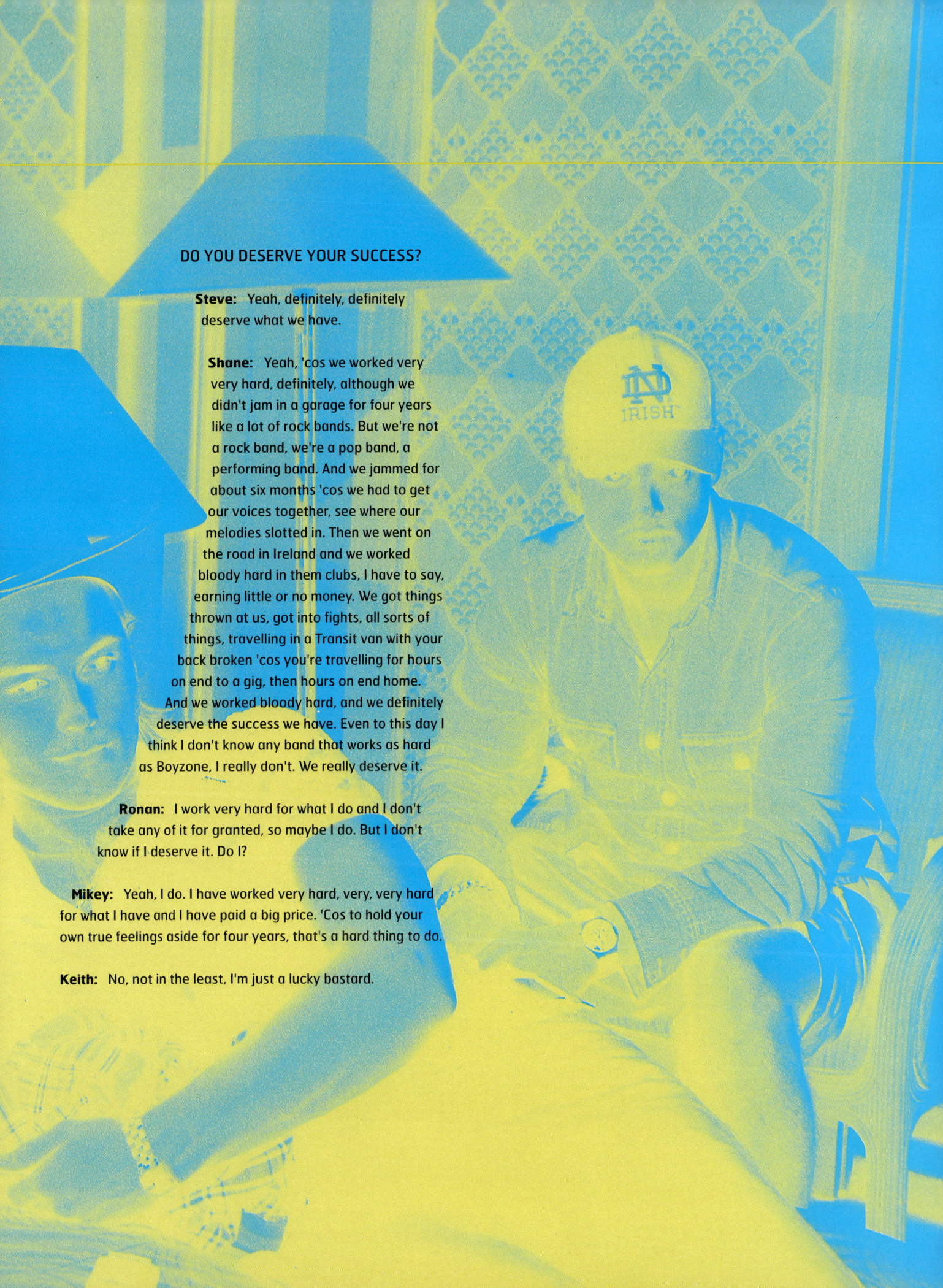

DO YOU DESERVE YOUR SUCCESS?

Steve: Yeah, definitely, definitely deserve what we have.

Shane: Yeah, 'cos we worked very very hard, definitely, although we didn't jam in a garage for four years like a lot of rock bands. But we're not a rock band, we're a pop band, a performing band. And we jammed for about six months 'cos we had to get our voices together, see where our melodies slotted in. Then we went on the road in Ireland and we worked bloody hard in them clubs, I have to say, earning little or no money. We got things thrown at us, got into fights, all sorts of things, travelling in a Transit van with your back broken 'cos you're travelling for hours on end to a gig, then hours on end home. And we worked bloody hard, and we definitely deserve the success we have. Even to this day I think I don't know any band that works as hard as Boyzone, I really don't. We really deserve it.

Ronan: I work very hard for what I do and I don't take any of it for granted, so maybe I do. But I don't know if I deserve it. Do I?

Mikey: Yeah, I do. I have worked very hard, very, very hard for what I have and I have paid a big price. 'Cos to hold your own true feelings aside for four years, that's a hard thing to do.

Keith: No, not in the least, I'm just a lucky bastard.

princess di

Taipei airport, Taiwan, having flown from the Philippines, Sunday 31st August.

It was on the TV news last night: "Princess Diana seriously hurt in car crash".

We're waiting at Taipei airport - with its signs warning that death is the penalty for drug smuggling - for Boyzone to get their visas, which for some reason have not yet been issued. There's a fair amount of restlessness, of twitching, of wanting to get to the hotel for a bit of rest.

Ronan's on the phone to a friend in New York. "Diana, Princess Diana, is dead" he says to the rest of the band, who are sitting on the floor beside immigration. Immediately you're amazed at how sad you feel. It's a surprise to know how much you're moved. Never even much liked the British royal family. All of Boyzone are stunned into silence.

Then Steve, his voice a whisper, says "I was going to be singing for her, at the premiere in London of the Disney film 'Hercules' ." He tugs at the shoelaces of his runners and lapses into silence again. The song Steve was going to sing, his song on the soundtrack, is called 'Shooting Star'.

Diana's death will follow the tour through South East Asia. Young lads on the road selling newspapers, in Seoul Jakarta and Surabaya, appear to haunt the windows of our cars. Di's face appears on magazine stands from Dubai to Bangalore.

That night at the '88 Olympic Tennis Arena in Seoul and at the next concert, at Dewan Wawasan in Kuala Lumpur in Malaysia, Boyzone stand in silence for one minute in tribute to Diana, bowing their heads. The audience, stilled with shared respect for this woman they did not know, honour her by joining Boyzone in this contemplative stillness. It's extraordinary, these frantic audiences calmed for a moment by the passing of time...

"Time is too slow for those that wait...
but for those that love, time is eternity." -
Lady Di's sister at Westminster Abbey.

WHAT'S THE BEST THING ABOUT BEING IN BOYZONE?

Ronan: Travel, friendship, witnessing cultures and people, opening your mind to a lot of things, a chance to sing and get paid for it, a chance to stand on stage and sing and have people scream. Music is the language of the world, everyone understands it no matter what language you speak.

Steve: Getting to see the world. I don't know any other 21 year old around my area of Dublin who's seen as much as I have in the past four years. I've seen an incredible lot, I've learnt about life, people.

Shane: I have personal feelings about that...

Mikey: Being a vital part of a machine that's admired by everyone, by lots of people.

Keith: Having so much admiration of other people, fans and stuff. Also, if you could imagine picking two or three of your best mates and being given the opportunity to travel the whole world with them and experience every different culture and most of your expenses paid, like a holiday that goes on forever... If Boyzone breaks up, if we never see each other for donkey's years, you can guarantee that somewhere around the world there will be one of Boyzone telling someone a story that's got to do with me. That's beautiful, noone can ever take that away from us. We'll never forget each other.

WHAT'S THE WORST THING ABOUT BEING IN BOYZONE?

Steve: It can be a bit of a pain getting up early in the morning.

Ronan: Getting up at 8 in the morning!

Mikey: Being an individual in a machine that the public think they own. They own the machine and the concept but they don't own the individual, that's the worst part.

Keith: Not getting to see your family as much as you'd like.

Shane: It's unpredictable. We know in our hearts where we want Boyzone to go. We work very, very hard for that but we don't exactly know if it's going to work for us. We've been very successful as of now but I don't know how much longer it's going to be successful. It's just very unpredictable and as your standards of living get higher you need to be earning more money and we're at a certain stage now where we do need to continue on, basically.

WHAT IS YOUR BIGGEST EXTRAVAGANCE?

Steve: I don't buy that much, I like to buy for others. I buy presents for me mum and dad and get things done to the house. If any of me family are ever stuck they know where to come. I haven't bought anything mad for myself. Bought a lap top computer for about £5,000.

Keith: Cars! I've been good now, I sold the Porsche before I came away on this trip and I got a sensible car, a BMW 325 (laughs), at least you can get the baby in the back, couldn't get the baby in the back of the Porsche.

Shane: What's extravagance mean? I've got me Porsche and me BMW and me truck and I've got all kind of materialistic things and the most bizarre one would be a gold chain. Anyone can spend forty grand on a car and it's not amazin', but when someone spends ten grand on a gold chain and bracelet, it's quite extreme. I'll own a tractor soon, a rock'n' roll tractor, full CD player, the lot. Me truck is a toy - when I was growing up me and me father used to watch Colt Seavers - the stunt man on TV - and he had a truck. I always said I wanted one of them when I was older. The first car I ever bought in me life was a pick-up truck when I was seventeen and I was the king around my area, I was the Don Juan. The truck I have now is a dream, it's not quite a monster truck yet it's a lot bigger than your average pick-up truck. It's raised and silver with a lot of chrome bars and it's got a stereo system worth about seven grand and it'd just blow your mind. It's a Toyota HiLuxe, a 4-door, a commercial vehicle not used for what I use it for - as looks - but to me it's just killer!

Mikey: I try not to go too overboard, I never have. I just bought a nice house which I like a lot 'cos I plan to make it my home. It's my palace and I haven't been in it much but I want to make it homely. In a few years I can see the kids running around the garden playing with the dogs and me feeling happy and relaxed . I reckon that that is the most extravagant thing I have. My car? BMW 318 IS Coupé.

Ronan: I spend a lot of money on clothes. If I saved all the money I spent on clothes I could have bought a house! It doesn't have to be a designer label so long as it fits but I like Prada, Donna Karan, Dolce & Gabbana. I bought a motorcycle recently, that was a bit of an extravagant thing for me to do. A Harley Davidson, wanted one since I was a kid, so it was a dream come true. Like Shane's Porsche, it's something I've always wanted.
BP: You were saying you love to get on your bike and put on your helmet and...
Ronan: Oh, there's nothing like a big wind in your face, the power of the bike. I don't drive fast, it's just cruising around at forty miles an hour. Mobile phone on and I can't hear it, the bikes too loud. Freedom man, like a bird in the sky.

shanty town, kuala lumpur, malaysia

Photo by Stephen Gately

Friday 5th September 1997.

Steve is walking through the shanty town behind the New World Hotel. The houses are rough and ready, elevated shacks thrown up with corrugated iron roofs. The people living here, the children playing in the dirt track, everyone seems so happy.

Look up from the shanty houses and you see the approaching 21st century, massive modern skyscraper edifices that tower around in a circle like hungry greedy gleaming monsters. A family invites us in for tea and cake. The man of the house, dressed in a sarong, tells us he has a cousin back in Dublin who's an accountant.

The children follow Steve, the shy and delighted young Pied Piper. You can see that he is moved, really touched by these glowing bright happy bubbling kids and the conditions they live in.

Each family is being paid $5,000 to move, we're told. A new house, a half-way decent one, costs $100,000 here. The land is already worth $280 a square foot.

In the distance not far away you can make out the outlines of the Twin Towers, the tallest building in the world. The air is heavy with the pollution that shades the atmosphere a grey monochrome.

Progress marches on. Each home here in shanty town has a number daubed on it, awaiting execution. The rumble of the earthmovers and the wrecking crew. This little shanty village gobbled up by the machine.

The youths here, they play football. Kids amble about. Two old ladies sit on some steps. A chicken clucks along with five baby chicklets wobbling along by her right leg.

The buildings are moving nearer.

backdoor men

You get used to going into hotels via the back entrance, being herded through kitchens and corridors unknown, being ushered into service elevators that carry you to a plush corridor somewhere.

Everything is done at a pace, a sort of breathless half-running pace.

BP: Last night you said you reckoned you wouldn't live to be 25...

Keith: I've been in three very serious car crashes and I survived them. If you saw the cars that I climbed out of...people have been killed in much lesser crashes. So I wasn't destined to die then. I'm not into Tarot cards and all that, but one girl told me my lifeline is cut in half and another one told me I'd be dead before I was 25. I don't dwell on it but when I'm pissed I always say that I'll be dead before I'm 25. It's not something I really believe...but it's always on me mind.

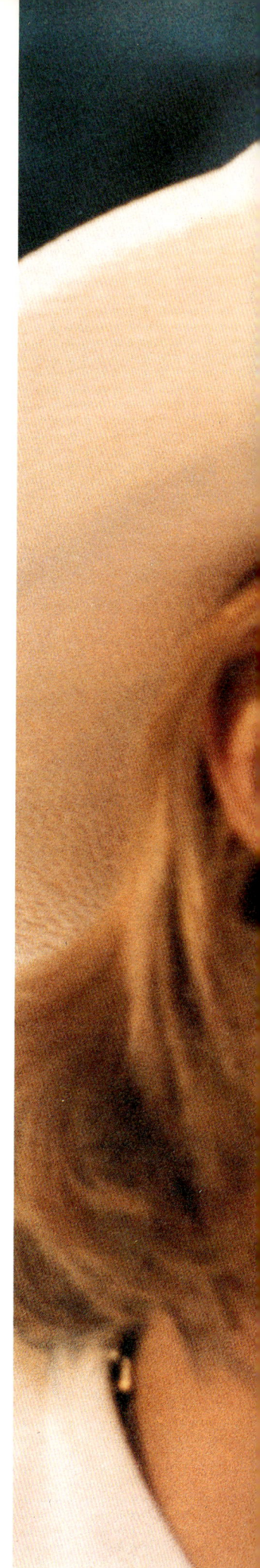

If the definition of class is generosity of spirit, Ronan has it. Whatever that indefinable thing is, Ronan Keating is a star. A star, plain and simple, no two ways about it. And suitably mad too.

ARE YOU A MENTLER?

Ronan: We're **all** mentlers! Just watch us go when we get together and go out on the tear! Yeah, we're mentlers. We're only human.

Keith: I get on well with people, enjoy meself, have fun, go out to clubs. I'm a mad bastard, a Jeckyll and Hyde. People meet me during the day and think "Pleasant enough chap, funny nice bloke". Then they go out with me and say "Who the **** is this mentler" 'cos I run amok. I'm just a mad whore, never regret a thing I do when I'm out, never remember the half of it. I probably drink too much. Being in Boyzone it's like every night is a Sunday night and every morning is a Monday morning!

NON JE NE REGRET RIEN

BP: Have you any regrets?

Ronan: No, **everybody** makes mistakes in their life and that's why they are what they are. I am who I am today because I made them mistakes. I'm happy with who I am. God made me make them mistakes, that's why I made them. So why would I change them?

BP: What kind of mistakes?

Ronan: I've made relationship mistakes, career mistakes. **Everybody** does that.

WHAT WOULD YOU LIKE TO HAVE THAT YOU DON'T?

Steve: For a person of my age I do have an awful lot. I think everyone deserves a chance, everybody deserves to do something different and have at least one dream to come true. I'd like to have that ability to be able to make a lot of wishes and dreams come true, to make people smile. I feel that, through kids saying "It was my dream to meet you" and me being just a normal person off the street, y' know. I sing, dance, I love singing and dancing, making some kid's dream come true...'cos there is so much badness in the world, there really is. There is more goodness than badness but people can be so cruel to each other. That's very sad and people do it without even realising and that's the even sadder thing. I couldn't physically hurt a person, I wouldn't be able to. I'm just not that type of person. I have hurt people, not physically, but Jesus how sorry I am for it. I think you do end up hurting people through your life. I wish I couldn't hurt anybody ever, I wish nobody could ever hurt me. That would be perfect.

Ronan: There's nothing 'Beep' I could ever wish for. That my family would be healthy - and they are thank God - that is the only thing I ever wish for. God bless us, your health is your wealth. If you haven't got it you've nothing, thank God we all have.

Shane: I've got everything. There is nothing I would like to have that I don't have, there is nothing...I know everything is comin' my way so I'm not in a hurry to have things. I know it's all comin', exactly what I want.

Keith: More time with me son and me loved ones.

Mikey: A deep sense of happiness and to be at peace, at one with meself, emotionally and spiritually within me soul. I long to find a soul mate, a woman who just loves me for what I am, for me. When all the chips are down she'll be my guiding light. They say that behind every strong and good man in the world is a good woman, and though I have all the strength and I have the exterior look, the one thing I am missing in life is the back-up of somebody great. But I think because of the way I am, I'm also afraid to find something like that - it can be taken away from you one day like everything in life can. That's why sometimes I'm afraid to have too much because it can be taken away so easily and there's nothing you can do about it. The only one true thing in life you always, always have and that can never be taken away from you is music, 'cos life, love and materialistic things can all be taken away. But if all the people you love and all the money in the world that you had, if everything was taken away from you, you can still sit there and write a song and sing about it. To me music is a way of emotional expression because I have a tough time expressing meself emotionally - I don't cry. Music is the only outlet for me, to let out what I feel, what I think, it's my way, it's the only thing I have really...

the bp boyzone q & a

IS THE PUBLIC FACE OF BOYZONE REAL?

Ronan: When people meet us they know, yes definitely, that we're as real as it gets. We're not namby pamby boys that jump around the stage, that don't write their songs and don't get involved when someone is telling them what to do. We're not puppets, we run the show, we enjoy what we do. There is no crap.

Steve: As real as it needs to be. People see us as people - more so now than ever, people are just seeing who we are, we're just normal people. Everyone gets into trouble, everyone drinks at some stage. You have to live, can't keep closed up in a nut shell, you have to get out and do things otherwise you'll crack up. We go out and have a laugh in the night or have a chat in the hotel or have a cry, we're only people, only living beings, not aliens. It can hurt...

Shane: It's very real but **unreal** in a sense that us as five lads, we do not at all hide any kind of reality about us. I have got a girlfriend, the lads have babies. The public know that we drink alcohol, we don't hide it from people, it's there in your face yet people still say we're clean cut teeny bopper. That's the public I think hiding things for us, making it unreal. We don't do that, we're just our own people, we do as we please. The public just change that for some reason.

Keith: Yeah, we don't pretend to be anything we're not, what you see is what you get. Boyzone fans know me, know exactly what I'm like. You get 400 girls standing outside every hotel in Britain when we're on tour in Britain and they see me at four or five in the morning pissed out of me face, having a great time, and they think it's great, they just think I'm a funny bastard, you know. The one time I had Lisa at Wembley and we stayed in the bar with Nigel Martin Smith, Take That's manager and I got pissed with him, totally locked. And Lisa was carrying me up to bed in the hotel and about five girls came into the hotel all dressed up and Lisa is holding me up in the lift and they stopped the lift doors and said "Keith, you're the real party animal, we need you at the party with us, come on, you can't go to bed!" I don't remember that now. Lisa says to me the next day "What have you been doing, everyone just knows you as the ****** party animal, every magazine I read you're just a nutter" and I say "No, I do my work, I'm very professional." I get on with everyone and when it comes to night time I make people laugh, make meself laugh, do funny things. I don't like sittin' down and drinkin', that's not being sociable. I like getting up and using the drink to the best of my ability and making people laugh and having a good time. That's drinking sociably, that's all I do.

Mikey: To a certain extent, we try to be as normal, as open as we can. It **is** fairly real but I think we have all become business minded too over the last four years and realised that in certain aspects of it you have to be a businessman. You are at the end of the day like any single band, whether it's Oasis, U2 or Boyzone. You're selling a product so you have to try and present the product in the best light that you can. So maybe sometimes, maybe 10% or 20% of the face isn't real, but most times we try to portray what we really are. You've got to contain **certain** things.

HOW IRISH A GROUP ARE BOYZONE?

Ronan: Muck slappers! Very Irish man! We have more Dublin accents than the people do at home. See, when we're away we don't want to lose them, we travel so much so we put them on when we're away – so when we come home we're even worse! Me Ma's going "Where did you get that from, your dits and your dats?" We all go home. We all love Dublin. We're talking about walking down Grafton Street and Henry Street. I love the winter in Dublin and O'Connell Street lit up with the lights. Fabulous.

BP: You were saying you don't get the recognition in Ireland...

Ronan: I think it's time they gave us a little more. Come on, we sell a lot of albums around the world, every interview we say we're Irish. Why can't we go home to our town and be welcomed and feel proud to be Irish? U2 can. We can sell more albums than them, than the Cranberries, any of them bands.

BP: Sell more albums than them?

Ronan: In some places, not everywhere. My country is important. What's the problem, are you jealous of us? We're proud to be Irish, let us **be** Irish, let us be welcome in our home, that's all we want. Went home to the IRMA's last February and picked up the best Irish band award but we didn't get the recognition that U2 or the Cranberries would have got. Pop music is one of the biggest markets of music in the world. We've opened the door in Ireland. There was only rock bands before then. All we want is a hello instead of a swear, a hand shake instead of two fingers in the air. What's the problem? We're not going to give you any hassle, we just want to enjoy ourselves and go home to the place we were born and raised.

Steve: Very Irish. Born and raised in Ireland, five Northsiders. How Irish can you get?

Mikey: Very.

Keith: I don't think you could get any Irisher, to be honest. We're typical Irish people but we're a bit more broad minded, we're a bit more cosmopolitan now. We don't think as Irish people anymore, we think as open minded, broad-minded people. We're more educated in the ways of the world, not academically but in living. A lot of us can speak on a one-to-one level to people they might have a high regard for, without feeling embarrassed. We've learnt to do that through all the interviews we've done throughout our time with the band.

Shane: Very Irish. **I'm** not very Irish. Maybe in the way I talk, but not in the way I think. Far from it, not even in a sense of dress or walk and talk. Irish people are very narrow minded and I'm talking in general 99%. I'll tell you one main thing I think about that – four years ago when I first got into this band I earned £50 a week. The five of us were talking about the money situation. £20,000 came up and the boys were ranting and raving about twenty grand, like it was all the money in the world. To me it's pocket change. Didn't have it then but now it's pocket change. It's not an Irish way to think higher than everybody. My father influenced me to set my sights high. And to this day a hundred grand is pocket change 'cos my money values have gone a lot higher. I think very differently...

WHAT'S THE BEST THING ABOUT YOU?

Ronan: I had a fantastic upbringing, great family. I'm an honest person, me mother never told me to lie, if I lied she'd know straight away.

Steve: That's not for me to say.

Shane: I'm honest. I only say something when I have something to say, otherwise I will keep me mouth shut. I don't crap on and on about things I don't know ab... just speak when I have something to say and that's a very good thing. Sometimes it upsets a lot of people 'cos I'm honest and I'm cold in what I say, I don't beat... the bush, that can get...not in trouble, but I can have conflict with the lads in the band. I would like to think that they appreciate it at the end of the day that I'm h... and straight up. As far as me mates are concerned, I'm a very good mate and I would do anything for anyone and I have done in the past. As far as females are concerned and the woman in my life is concerned, I think I'm a very, very lovable person. I would die for her.

Mikey: I don't know. Maybe four years ago I could have written you a book about the best things about me, now I don't know, don't know if I have one good th... about me. I don't know...

Keith: I have a big heart.

WHAT'S THE WORST THING ABOUT YOU?

Ronan: (long pause) Being paranoid probably. Wish I wasn't.

Steve: My body is not in good shape - paranoid about it, very much - other people can answer this.

Shane: As far as me mates are concerned, I can be a little bit cold. As far as feelings are concerned, I don't express my feelings, I'm not an emotional person. If someone gave me a gift, thanks, even though deep down in side I am so happy but I don't express that, don't know why, that's just me. As far as females would be concerned I'm such a jealous person it's unreal, unreal. It's because I am a bloke, I know how blokes think...and I know good and bad, I'm a very good judge of cha... And if someone gets friendly with the wrong person I'm an anti Christ, you just don't get in me way 'cos I will go through somebody - when it comes to females yo... to be careful.

Mikey: I could write you a book on that, we'd be here all night.

Keith: I have a big heart.

WHAT'S THE BEST THING ABOUT BP FALLON?

Ronan: He's a world of different things, different aspects. I met him a couple of years ago and listened to him from the first time I met him and was very interes... what he had to say. Warm person, very caring, knows what he wants in life, very open mind and try anything once. He has many years under his belt but he has a ... heart, he's a wonderful man, I've a lot of love for him.

Steve: His stories, his experiences, he has lived the life and I think he's lived a good life. Very genuine. I don't trust many people and I think I could trust him if I h... something to say and I asked him not to I don't think he would. There's not many people I feel comfortable with in that way. He's also a bit of a lunatic, bit mad, b... everything, bit of Einstein, bit of Gene Kelly rolled in one.

Shane: I think he's mad, very wise, things he's seen, things he's done is very, very interesting, amazes me quite a lot, I like to listen to his stories, such an outgoi... man, no cares in the world, got the biggest bollix in the world of anyone I have ever known, just lives life to the full.

Mikey: To me he has two sides. He's two men. One man I actually think is cool, a nice fellow, very lovable, gentle, kind, and charismatic. He's thoughtful of every... and does a lot for everybody and should be admired for his hard work and for the way he thinks sometimes. He has a lot of answers, and a lot of wisdom, but he h... another side to him too...

Keith: He has a big heart.

Photo by Suraj Jagan

WHAT'S THE WORST THING ABOUT BP FALLON?

Ronan: Eh, sometimes he's too flippin' carefree, too easy going...

Steve: He's a bit sensitive at times, not as sensitive as me but sensitive at times. I don't see that as a bad point really, don't see that as the worst, worst thing about him. I don't think there is anything that bad, a person is a person, people have their faults.

Shane: He can be a bit much at times 'cos he's so hyper - when we're bollixed he can be like "Come on lads, let's do this, that", we go "Leave it out!".

Mikey: Could write a book on it, be here all night! Only joking! You don't want to know what I think. It's not really nice to hear the bad side of a person. Who am I to sit here and tell about anybody's faults? I am nobody's judge and jury and nobody is mine - though every single human being wants to be that, they're not. Who has any God given right above another person to say or give out about bad faults? I too am guilty of doing that at times, like everyone, I'm only human. But when I'm in a calm humour I can see wisdom. It's not right to judge anybody. We all have our faults. One day we'll all pay for them...

Keith: He has a big heart.

Photo by Claire De La Luna

WHAT'S THE LAST LIE YOU TOLD?

Ronan: (Laughing) All that crap I said about BP Fallon!

Mikey: I don't know. I try not to lie too often...

Steve: I tell fibs but just for a laugh, for practical jokes. I wouldn't tell a serious lie.

Shane: I lie every day of my life. Well, I don't think I actually **lie**. We do questions in interviews as Boyzone and one of the main questions always is "Do you have girlfriends?" If the question is about me I will say "Yes I do", but if the question is about the band...

Keith: Oh Jesus, it was probably about the amount of drink I drank!

the great boyzone cigarettes controversy

Jakarta, Indonesia, Monday September 8th 1997.

It ended like any Boyzone press conference. Except at the end Phil, who had flown out from England to take some pictures for Boyzone and their fan magazine, handed the band a packet of Mild cigarettes. The cigarette packets were printed with Boyzone's name on them, with the Boyzone logo, with Boyzone's photographs, with the titles of Boyzone hits 'A Different Beat' and 'Words' and 'A Picture of You'.

"These were being handed out to the journalists and the photographers," Phil announces.

The band are freaked, even the guys who smoke ciggies, truly disturbed at the idea of handing out cigarettes with Boyzone's image endorsing them. Mark Plunkett hides the packets from you, won't let you see them. He knows you'll write about it.

"If they find out about this back home and in England, we're in trouble," says Keith.

Turns out that Mild are one of the sponsors for the Indonesian leg of the tour. They're planning to hand out the cigarettes at the gig, hand them out to the youngsters who have come to see Boyzone. "In the contract, it says that we have to be informed of who the sponsors are - but we weren't," says Mark.

The scheme by Mild to feed the young Boyzone audience with Boyzone cigarettes is banged on the head by Mark on behalf of the band, who has to fight for his territory. We're told that the cigarettes would be destroyed but it's a hollow victory. The next night at Bengkel Night Park in Jakarta, where Boyzone are forced to leave the stage for some ten minutes while the crush in the audience is sorted out, the venue is literally dripping in Mild promotional material, Mild promotional material that says "Mild Live: Ronan, Steven, Shane, Keith and Mikey, Let's Make A Different Beat."

To make matters worse, you've turned up in an unsubtle t-shirt bearing the message "CIGARETTES KILL. DON'T GIVE MILD TO THE CHILD". In the dressing room before the show, Ronan is saying "What should we do? What **can** we do?" and you're suggesting "Go on stage and rip up the cigarettes in front of everybody and say 'Look, this has nothing to do with us, we don't support it.'" "I'll have to think about it" says Ronan, upset.

Boyzone do nothing.

Two concerts away, in Bali, in a gorgeous ampitheatre adorned by strange magnetising figures of gods and deities and swirling patterns, before the soundcheck Iain Whitehead discovers a large lit up Mild Cigarettes packet five foot high at each side of the stage. He asks for it to be moved. Nothing happens.

He mentions that maybe these cigarette displays are costly, that maybe they might get broken if they aren't taken away immediately. The glowing cigarette packets disappear.

After Jakarta, Boyzone play in Surabaya in the Go Skate Building. As Boyzone come off stage before the encore, dripping, Mark is standing there, his arms overflowing with packets of Boyzone cigarettes. "They were handing these out in the audience," Mark says.

Boyzone go back on stage and rip up the cigarettes in front of the audience and say "Look, this has nothing to do with us. We don't support it."

Photo by Baron Beetmoll Troy

a different beat

w o r d s

picture of you

boyzone

A Different

Indonesia - Se

SAMPOERNA

36 %

97/98

WHAT'S YOUR MOST THRILLING EXPERIENCE SO FAR?

Keith: First day I bought me Porsche, great feeling, about a year ago. I didn't think I'd own any type of car and driving down the road in a nice flash Porsche, everyone looking at you, feels good! (laughter)

Ronan: Four years of this has just been an exhilarating, fantastic time, a rollercoaster ride of music, fun, tears and laughter and sorrow and joy. Please God it goes on.

Steve: God I've had many. Probably doing the Disney song has to be the most thrilling. The Andrew Lloyd Webber song is very thrilling for me too, just great that I've got the opportunity that I've been given, it's called 'No Matter What', it's a beautiful song.

Mikey: The birth of me daughter. It was a beautiful one but a strange one. It was hard for me to comprehend because I've been away and travelling on the road all the time. Though I knew in me mind I had a child on the way, being the youngest of a family and never experienced having anyone younger than me to look after, it was hard for me to come to terms with it. I didn't know what to do really but the experience of the birth was overwhelming, really, really overwhelming. And when she was born I held her in my arms and it just touched me. Her name is Hannah.

Shane: Being born - I couldn't ask for any more than that really.

BIGGEST FEAR

Ronan: Snakes, hate them things. I'll get over them one day. My biggest fear is being unsuccessful in the music industry. It would kill me. I've worked too hard to let it go.

Keith: Having become accustomed to this lifestyle, if the band came to an end...I wouldn't be able to give my son the lifestyle he has already. I'm frightened that I might lose everything.

Steve: Losing anybody really close to me.

BP: Have you ever?

Steve: Yeah I've lost a lot of people. If it was any of my close family I'd go mad, me mum or dad. It's going to happen some day but that's a fear that everyone has, losing parents. But you got to learn how to deal with it. There are plenty of fears. Fear of a gun being pointed at you, fear of not getting success for a song that you like, fears in everything.

Mikey: I don't fear anything except fear itself. That's my biggest fear.

Shane: I don't fear an awful lot. I don't fear death. I wouldn't like to die but I don't fear it. If I'm going to die I'm going to die. If God said "Eh...take him off the earth," that's life.

the opium den, taipei, taiwan

Monday 1st September, 1997

Mikey is the tail of the dragon, the odd one out. Even in his
body language, he seems removed. Everybody sits in the
misleadingly-named Opium Den disco in Taipei, all sitting in
a little alcove under what looks like the
velvet roof of some Arabic
prince's tent.

Everyone's vibing, whacking in
the ol' loosening juices. Keith is
in full blab, telling you about
his vibe on girls. And himself.
Duster, they call him, the
clown of the group.
Thoughtful too, sometimes.
Warm man, mad and mad
for it. Crazy for his son,
"Crazy for me bird Lisa."
Spends a fortune calling
her back home in Dublin.

Mikey's in the middle of all
this verbal, people
shouting and laughing
and clanking glasses and
telling each other how
much they love each
other. Whole lotta
hugging going on.
But Mikey's in another
stratosphere, his hands
clasping his knees, focused
on another world.

You touch him on the
shoulder. "It'll be alright" he
says. "I'm just trying to figure
it out."

Then everyone gets up and
shakes a tail feather to
Grandmaster Flash and Melle Mel
ripsnorting their way through
their wild rap classic 'White Lines'.

AB FAB! PHOTO BY RONAN KEATING

AND WHAT WAS THE BEST MOMENT ON THIS TOUR?

Keith: For me it was Bali, great experience, that swimming pool area, some laughs. Hong Kong was ****** great fun, great night that night in the disco! Bahrain was beautiful, out in the speed boat. Perfect.

Mikey: This interview is very interesting. I like doing interviews. Bahrain was a nice place, a nice beach, sun, beautiful hotel, good vibe.

Shane: The best for me was Bahrain, where I went water skiing. I used to do it with my da and family and that took me back to what I used to be. And that will be a memorable moment for me 'cos I felt real again.

Ronan: Had some laughs, went out a few nights, had some great times. Last night was a fantastic show in India, other side of the world and 9,000 people want to hear our songs. They know who Ronan Keating is and who Shane Lynch and Boyzone are. Wow! Fantastic.

Steve: Sitting on a beach in Bahrain with three friends. I'll always remember that, that's one for my books from my life. We sat down, me, BP Fallon, Ronan and Shane, three good friends of mine and we sat down and chatted about the world and life and anything and everything. It was lovely, really relaxing for me. I felt really good, listening to the water coming up, rubbing my toes into the sand. Fantastic.

WHAT WAS THE WORST MOMENT ON THIS TOUR?

Keith: I can't remember the half of it! There wasn't really any bad sides on the tour.

Steve: Me getting sick, not being able to perform as well as I'd like on the last night in Bangalore....

Shane: It's been a long journey, with a bit of hard work, but I can't complain. I choose to be here.

Ronan: Coming to the end we all got a bit lost. Everybody got mentally tired. When you're coming to an end of a tour your body is saying to you "I need a rest". We've a couple of days off before we go to France.

BP: Tell us what happened when we arrived here today?

Ronan: It was scary, thousands of people. We have people who are paid to look after us, them people don't, they get hurt. It scares me. Someone told them we were coming and they shouldn't.

Mikey: The worst point was probably here in India just as we arrived in the hotel, here in Bombay. I'm never that way but I got very very nervous 'cos there were so many people both outside and inside the hotel and there was only Barry looking after the five of us. It looked like it could at any stage explode. There was no back-up for us.

"Though he should live a hundred years, not seeing the Truth Sublime; yet better, indeed, is the single day's life of one who sees the Truth Sublime." – quote from 'The Teaching of Buddha, given to BP Fallon by the manager of the Marco Polo Hotel, Singapore.

Even the guy manning the x-ray machine at the airport in Cebu is filming, videoing the guys getting ready to fly to Manila. There's fans a go go. Pens and papers waving in the air. Cameras click click clickety click. The ever-present vigil.

At the airport in Jakarta there's Boyzone mania. Boyzone are stashed in the men's toilets while their excavation is plotted by the powers that be. Finally a human rope of policemen lassoes the fan fodder and pushes it through the exploding crowd. Hands stretch out and now someone's grabbed Ronan by the hair. He goes down, knocked over by the rush and the pushing and the weight of bodies. Barry Knight leans down and cradles the stunned singer, cutting his way through the screaming out of control worshippers.

Barry and cargo, hotly pursued by wailing fanatics, make it into the open where he stuffs Ronan into a waiting Mercedes that speeds him away from the clawing crowd.

In Bombay where the band have flown after their final gig of the South East Asia tour, 9,000 crazed Boyzone fans, young men in cheeky "Hello, Boyze" t-shirts holding hands and younger girls going mental in Bangalore. In Bombay the band arrive at the famed Taj Mahal Hotel to find the streets thronged with thousands of people, young and old. One policeman trying to hold back the crowd is beating a little old lady on the ankles with a stick. The little old lady falls down.

Boyzone make a run for it into the lobby only to be thrown back by the expanding welcoming crowd.

Back into the cars. Round the back in through the kitchens. Up through the service elevator. Safety. "That was frightening" says Steve. "It's not even us I'm worried about - there's people could get hurt, people could get trampled." Later, Boyzone are being interviewed by TV stations on the roof of the Taj Mahal Hotel with the historic Gateway Of India in the background. Down in the surrounding streets the fans call out for Ronan, Steve, Shane, Keith and Mikey.

"And how do you find India?" the TV interviewer asks the famous five.

This most gentlemanly of gentlemen Mark Plunkett the tour manager is losing it. "Get off this floor or I'll throw you out of the window!" he blurts out, completely uncharacteristically, as the startled Hong Kong fans scuttle back to the elevators.

Only on one other occasion does Mark snap. It's on the plane from Bangalore to Bombay. Boyzone are trying to get on the plane. Soon as a Boyzone head reaches the top of the steps from the tarmac and sticks his face into the aircraft he's engulfed in shrieking teens, thrusting bits of paper and pushing and the recipient of their overwrought attention's out of the plane again. It's Bedlam, airhostesses surrendering to the mania, either standing around in it or grabbing paper too and joining the clamouring throng. Madness.

Keith tries to, well... push his way back in. It's like trying to get a Camel through the eye of a needle. Forget it. This isn't happening. There's no refuge anywhere. If this is love—give me comfort, somewhere to, y'know, chill out. "Wheeeew!" The fans, they emote wild cries that signal an amphetamine-like enthusiasm that is unable to grasp that maybe, well, that maybe their idols need a little peace now and then. These fans, they just want a little piece too. Screaming. Autographs...

"Just bloody sit down, all of you" Mark commands, the patriarchal schoolteacher mentally fogging up behind his glasses.

Taipei airport, Tuesday 2nd September 1997

Arriving at Taipei airport to fly to the next concert, in Seoul in Korea, Ro lifts his head to the one-way windows of the space wagon. Outside there's a wondrous lunacy, fans a go go, crazed. Taking in this glorious madness, Ro notes sleepily "Our luggage hasn't arrived yet. There's time for five minutes more sleep."

Shane, who actually goes to bed at night, clambers out to sign autographs and pose for pictures with the delirious fans, who burst into even wilder exhilaration. Inside the relative calm of the space wagon which cradles them like a protective womb, Ronan, Steve and Keith do the horizontal boogie, trying to catch a few more precious zzzzzs...

For a split second it's some mad Satyricon freeze-frame, the girls shook into silence, just standing there disarmed.

Keith's Bambi eyes relax.

The fans huddle back to their seats, almost chastised, ready to reactivate themselves for a second strike as Mark shepherds the rest of the Boyz on to this strange plane.

You're talking to Keith during the flight and in ones and twos now these fans tippitoe and giggle to where we are, and Keith signs.

We're talking so much that we miss the heart-stopping sight of the world's biggest shantytown, which we fly over as we prepare to land in Bombay.

SIGNING SESSIONS

Signing sessions are part of the Boyzone life. Boyzone, they've a good vibe towards it, seem to genuinely enjoy meeting their fans. Once, when Boyzone had a signing session at the Virgin Megastore in London, the whole street was closed off - the first time ever - and the police insisted that Boyzone cancel their appearance, for the sake of public safety.

All over South East Asia, the Middle East and India, from Kuala Lumpur to Hong Kong to Bahrain to Bombay, excitable girls clutching Boyzone paraphernalia throng into some sort of queue, sobbing and laughing, jostling and pushing and every now and then raising their faces to the heavens to emit random screams.

The boys sit behind a desk and the fans appear from the left, with a gift or a picture to be signed or a camera or, more likely, all three. In patient conveyor belt fashion, the guys pass the stuff to be signed down the line as the eager receiver moves from band member to band member, rushing off bearing the autographs with swoops of joy or overcome with tears at the adrenaline of it all.

In Bahrain, the signing outside the Diesel shop has to be abandoned when the crowd gets out of control. Mark signals the guys and suddenly they leap up and they're sprinting to the waiting cars. Steve stumbles into a chair that's been pushed into his path in some strange attempt by the fans to slow his disappearance. Barry, in one balletic movement like a cross between Rudolf Nureyev and Muhammad Ali, leans forward and steadies Steve while at the same time propelling him forward, all hurtling onwards through the shopping mall to the sanctuary of the waiting cars, which propel them back to the hotel, sweating and laughing.

The runners, it's for the safety of the fans. Too many people and it's in danger of exploding, of young people getting hurt. It's better to leave. After each concert, as the closing music to Boyzone's song 'A Different Beat' hovers in the air, Ronan, Steve, Shane, Keith and Mikey race from the venue and shoot into the vehicles that speed them away, more often than not guided by a police motorcycle escort with sirens blazing. The guys sit back in the seats, wiping themselves with towels and glugging on plastic bottles of cold water, exhausted.

In Bombay, the signing, held in the hotel disco with Boyzone sitting behind the same long table they'd earlier sat behind for their press conference, is stopped by the hotel manager even though the conduct of the fans is less frenetic than usual. Ronan grabs the microphone from the freaked out hotel manager and shouts " It's not us that's stopping this!" and exits to cheers from the cheated crowd.

Taipei, Taiwan, Monday September 1st and Singapore. Monday September 8th 1997.

In Taipei, Shane and yourself, we adventure to the Lung Shan temple, where multi-coloured fruits are laid out for the gods and deep red candles in gold urns burn brightly to the infinite spirits. On the roof, awesome and elaborate dragons stand guard.

In Singapore, we journey on to the Sri Thandayuthapani temple on Tank Road, with its beautiful and inspiring Hindu shrines and a courtyard roofed by forty-eight engraved glass panels angled to catch the rising and setting suns.

We continue on, round the corner to Race Course Road, to the Temple Of A Thousand Lights. There, a fifteen metre high statue of Buddha with gold fingers beams down on us, enigmatic and benign. Big Buddha is watching you.

Manama, Bahrain, Wednesday 17th September 1997.

It's the night after the lunar eclipse and we sit there on the beach, warm in the brightness of the moon. If the sun is the mother of life, then the moon is the mistress of mystery.

We sit in a line on chairs in the sand, Ronan, Steve, Shane and yourself. The talk is all fairly cosmic, about the moon and the stars and the meaning of life.

Shane and Steve get to talking ghost stories, real ones, each outdoing the other in these ghastly tales.

Ro's got his head back in his chair and he's looking up at the sky and he's lost to another world, in awe of the everlastingness of space and time.

Steve's gabbing away. "And another story..." he starts again and Ro catches his mate Steve chatting away seven to the half dozen. "And another story" and Ro jolts upright and cracks up at Steve launching into another yarn when there's the whole universe out there to ponder.

Then Ro's got his head back again, tilted right back, night dreaming, night beaming, gazing upwards at infinity with the caress of wonderment.

The talk turns to which animal you'd like to be, with Steve favouring being a dolphin and Ro electing to be an eagle. The discussion evolves into whether there's more space to swim or more space to fly.

Right at that moment out of left field, Keith crashes into view. "Look at the state of you" he says. "Yis are all **gone**". Holding firmly onto his glass, he navigates his way back through the night and lies down on a sunbed near Tim the guitar player and Paul Turner the Boyzone bassist who, let it be known, once backed rock 'n' roll icon Chuck Berry, Chuckleberry the king of the cunning lyrics and guitar ringing like a bell.

Keith wakes up beside the swimming pool at four in the morning, wakes up to a deserted world in the light of a new day beginning...

marc

Watching the rippling reflection of the full moon in the sea by the sand on the Gulf of Bahrain, thinking of you.

It was twenty years ago today – well yesterday, actually – when you died. You're still one of my best friends, a cheeky rock'n'roller who pulled heart strings and weaved spells and made the little girls scream.

It was a gas. "Life's a gas" you sang, and it was and it is.

God, it was magic.

Manama, Bahrain, Thursday September 18th 1997.

Dawning in Bahrain and Ronan rings you at 6.30 in the morning. "Are you awake?" he says and actually yes you are and so off you go for a wander on the open beach, already warm from the rays of the new rising sun.

There's no-one about, just a few strange fish about six inches long like thin swimming hot dogs that follow us as we stroll the beach.

There's magic in the air. Clarity. A translucent light.

On a little island reached by a stone causeway there are luscious tropical plants, greener and cleaner than a Disney fantasia. On the beach, a solitary man rakes up the seaweed. That seems to be his job. To tidy up the beach. He seems gently amazed to see two people wandering around at this time of the day. This man, he's raked the whole of the beach, delicate undulating lines patterning their way across the sand and into the tickling waters. Ronan's footprints tell him he's walking on this man's work, destroying a creation worthy of Fellini or Salvador Dali.

Suddenly aware of the destruction he's causing, Ronan bows to the man and says "I'm sorry sir."

The man continues raking seaweed.

Our footprints lead us to where we are.

Taiwan, Sunday 31st August 1997.

Driving in Taiwan - headed for Taipei from the airport. Ro chews his fingers in the back of the car, white cowboy hat on his head. Watery rice paddy fields and little men in lampshade hats whizz by the window.

Ro's talking about Boyzone going to Indonesia. Back home, there's been a big controversy in the Irish newspapers giving out to Boyzone for going there. Considering the things we're told that Indonesia did in East Timor. Hundreds and thousands of people were murdered.

"If I had my way, I wouldn't be going there" Ro is saying. "In Berlin these two chaps came to see us, we had a meeting. One had lost both his parents and the other had lost four brothers. It's heartbreaking. I don't claim to know the whole story, that I'm educated in it. But you **know** when something is wrong..."

Hong Kong, Monday September 15th 1997.

You're sitting there in Hong Kong in your room at the hotel, which is imaginatively titled 'The Hong Kong Hotel'. Ronan 's here, and Steve and Boyzone guitarist Tim. Tim, it's his first-ever professional gig on the road, first time out. First time into the vibes and the madness. Tim's the root of rock 'n' roll in all this, the man whose nightly guitar solo in the Boyzone song 'Paradise' brings it home that Boyzone are a pop group but a pop group with a rock 'n' roll heart. Tim, he's a mainline twanger.

In the corridors outside, girls prowl up and down looking for a Boyzone. Round the corner where Boyzone are quartered, guards sit on chairs for twenty four hours a day.

Anyways...you're in your room writin' this song titled 'Lie To Me'. "Lie to me, tell me you love me" it goes, and Ronan says it's like a Bon Jovi song. Oh dear. At your request, Ro throws in some of his own lines. "Another fire on another night, so give me a toke of that pipe" Ronan freeforms. He thinks for a minute, then says, laughing "It's not a **Boyzone** song!"

Bombay

Bombay is an overdose of information that assaults you, that pummels into your head and your heart and your soul and leaves you drained and gaspin' yet adrenalised by the spirituality of these people, spirituality is all that they've got.

At night, semi-clad children asleep on the pavement, their bodies coiled on the ground like sleeping dogs. People sleeping on the eighteen inches of concrete that divides the traffic lanes. People wearing rags. Little kids, naked, playing beside an open sewer and a dead rat, happy as piglets in shite, bless their hearts, the lambs of the world unaware of the pitfalls ahead. "Oh to be a child again, to feel the freedom of the wind..."

It hurts seeing all of this.

But what the blues is, the blues heals.

And elevates.

and we all shine on

WHERE WILL YOU BE IN TEN YEAR'S TIME?

Shane: I'll definitely be married. I hope to have four or five kids..

Ronan Hopefully still doing a book with you BP somewhere!
Maybe we'll be in the North Pole doing a tour up there man,
(laughing), and you're going to write another book. Who knows? I'll
definitely be singing, this is all I've ever known how to do and ever
been successful at. I love doing it.

Steve I have no idea. I do know I'd like to have a place in Dublin,
one in London, one in New York and just work within the business,
creating music, maybe acting...
BP: Musicals?
Steve: I'll aim for a solo career first before I go do a musical. I'd
love to try everything.

Keith: I have no idea. I believe I'm destined to do something
else. Boyzone is not the highlight of me whole life. If I live till I'm 60
or 80 that's 50 years talking about memories 'cos nothing will
ever top this. Still, I really believe that something else is going to
top this, that this is just a stepping stone for me. I've taken pride in
every job I've ever done. Boyzone is very difficult for me to take
pride in me work 'cos somebody has written better songs than me,
sings better than me, dances better than me, answers questions at
interviews better than me, looks better, dresses better. So there's
nothing in the group that I can say is my little baby. But that's not a
problem. I love the band to bits but there is something out there
that I have to be able to do and I'll look back on it and say I done
that and it was good.

Mikey I don't know why but I see meself as being married with more
children and very very happy. Completely in control of meself on a
professional level. Not being afraid but having the freedom to be me
in every aspect, musically and whatever. I see meself finding
happiness and peace within meself, just a calmness about meself,
being fulfilled and completed. I'm definitely not completed now, no way.

'Instant Karma' on 'Top Of The Pops', London England Feb 11th 1970.

Shane: Very clever. They were one of the biggest bands in the world, and if John Lennon said "It's only a group that ****** broke up" it shows you how down to earth and level headed they stayed. Fair play.

Ronan: Lennon said that about the Beatles when they broke up. In his eyes they had a good time, they had a laugh, travelled around the world, one of the biggest boy bands ever and I guess one day someone was going on "Oh my god you're from the Beatles!"...and he obviously turned around and said "Will you shut up for God's sake! All we were was a band that broke up." You can understand that.

BP: Could that relate to Boyzone?

Ronan: I think we will be remembered more for being here than not being here.

Steve: Told his fans "It's not the end of the world, plenty more bands around, the music will still live on". You've got the music, the band are still around, they're not dead. The band broke up but there are plenty more things to live for and you will always have the music, the memories.

BP: Could that relate to Boyzone?

Steve: Yes, definitely.

Keith: Ah ****** great, perfect. I mean for him to be able to turn around and say that after being in The Beatles for so long, so successful, travelling the world, experiencing amazing things, to turn around and say "It's only a ***** group that broke up" means that he stayed with his two feet fully on the ground and that is respect to him. If it's over it's over, **** it, it was only a group that ****** broke up. I'd like to think meself when this band breaks up, "Good times, had a great laugh but **** it, it's over". I'll give us two years, I would love to say ten but, two years. If Boyzone breaks up ...fans not buying their records anymore, then it's time to break up. We won't ever let that happen. When we start going downhill I think we will know to say "That is it". If Boyzone breaks up before its time, in other words when the members can't live with themselves anymore, I will be very sad if that happens. It could happen, could happen right now but anything is possible, you never know what's around the corner. See, if everyone remembers that they're lucky and they don't take it for granted and they respect it, then we can stay together for a long time. But if anyone starts getting a little bit above themselves 'cos they've got a few quid in the bank and they got a lot of people recognising them as somebody important and they're getting well looked after in places that they go and they let it drift a little bit to their heads... as long as everyone remains with their two feet on the ground and doesn't read and believe their own press, they could stay together for ages. As long as everybody stays with their feet on the ground...

Mikey: I think he's dead right. At the end of the day they're all only flesh and blood and they all only pluck strings and press piano notes and hit drums and sing. Millions and millions of people all over the world can do it, The Beatles just happened for some reason to be picked from obscurity and they were plucking the right strings at the right time.

FINAL WORDS TO THE WORLD...

Ronan: Thank you to most of the world for accepting Boyzone for what we are. The world is a fantastic place let's keep it fantastic. Been to Bali, stunning, Dubai and it was scary, been to Bombay and it was scarier but that's what the world is all about, without the good you don't have the bad, without the scary you don't have the nice, so let's look after it, this beautiful world. Thank you and God bless you all.

Steve: Live your life, be happy, take care of the ones you love, don't worry until it's going to happen. Strive to be happy and in hundred years time who will care, who will give a ****. God bless the world and take care of the earth 'cos it's what your children will inherit.

Shane: The rest of the world is out there and I know where I stand. I stand in my own mind and thoughts and in what I'm going to achieve and the world is not going to get in my way. The world is a powerful place but I'm not asking for too much...

Keith: To the fans, thanks for giving Keith Duffy the opportunity to do what he's done. I never thought I'd get this opportunity, and the chance to see and experience the things that I've experienced. Thanks to them for giving me the opportunity to have the life I have.

Mikey: You ain't seen nothin yet, watch this space!

"Dream in the present, not the future "

THANX

This book is dedicated to my Godson Danny Dennehy
and all the children of the world, whatever our ages.
To Patricia Fallon with love and immeasurable gratitude.
Patsy Dennehy.
Annette Tallon.
Ronan Drury.
Graham de Courcy Wheeler.
Anne McDevitt.
Dan Egan at The Hairbox and Orla for 'The Lonely Planet'.
Ronnie Drew and Deidre
Mr Michael O'Keeffe and Maura.
Donal O'Malley and Anne.
Donal MacNally and Deirdre.
In India, Suraj and Sharmila.
In Surabaya, Nefransjah and Nefrianoora.
In Bali, Maarten Hubbeling and The Princess and Mr. SCTV himself.
James Wright - to be a rock and not to roll!?
Vanessa Gilbert and Ray Rubio in L.A. Joe King Carrasco in Texas.
Bill Kates in NYC. Ian Marriott+TJ+Bubbah in Atlanta.
Rachel Murray. Jenny Oman. Sarah Murray. Fiachna O'B.
Rovena Cardiel, David and little Isabella Luna.
Ronnie Wood and Jo Howard and Sherry Daly
Poppy Lloyd.
Stevo and the phunksters at Tower Records, Dublin.
Nigel, Frankie and Clem. Miya Debbie and Chris.
Aengus Fanning. And, naturally, Eamon Dunphy Willie Kealey, Liam
Collins, Campbell Sharp, John Chambers, Eamonn Butler. Anne Harris.
Sharon. Brian Farrell
and Tony Gavin.
Parachutes by Steven McGrath and Gabrielle O'Kelly and Beth E.Dean.
Paul Hewson and Paul McGuinness.
Patti Palladin and Anita Pallenberg. Marianne Faithfull
Pulse Fitness Centre, Temple Bar, Dublin.
Local Cabs, Dundrum. Sean Curley, Budget Rent A Car, Drumcondra.
Business Affairs Maitre D - Alan Duffy at OJ Killkenny and Co, Dublin.
Photographic Representation - Mark Bannister at Reaction, London.
Hi to Andy, Colin, Anita and Lucy. Hiya to Alan McGee and Noel G.
Literary Agents - Ross Edwards and Helenka Fuglewicz
at Edwards Fuglewicz, London.
Legal Representation - James O'Malley, O'Malley+Co., NYC.
Word processing by the wonderful Valerie Stevenson. Tea and
sympathy by Gerry. More processing by Joan Coughlan. Even more
processing by Noreen Donovan. And mo' by Noreen. And mo'. Yo!
Photography - b/w printed by the still virtually unreal and
fabberoonie Declan Barney Barnes at Kevin Dunne's Studio, Dublin. "
Play the blues, Hedge!" Thanx too to Stuart Smyth. Fujicolor by the
truly superfab Neasa De Cleir. Thanx too to Mick at Photo Labs,
Dublin.
Canon Eos Elan, Canon Eos 1000 NF, Canon lenses, Olympus Stylus,
Fujifilm Neopan 1600, Fujicolor 800 G Superplus, Sony M-529V
Microcassette-corder. Batteries not included. Felt pens and scribble
pads from Eason's, Dublin.
Art Direction by the incredible Steve Averill and Collages by the cool
John Brohy, Design by the brilliant Siobhán O'Carroll at ABA, Dublin.

Claire De La Luna.
Philip Dodd for carpeting the highway.
The indefatigable Hannah MacDonald. And Nicky
and Anna and all at Andre Deutsch.

Michelle Duffin, Sarah and Marnie at Trinifold Travel.
Louis Parker, Boyzone's agent who looks like John Mayall. Nigel Peters.
The Boyzone band - Paul Turner, Richie Taylor, Guy Richman and the
big twang himself Tim Pearson. Sarah Hollis on Boyzone Wardrobe.
Big shout out to Iain Whitehead and his crew - Matt Rosser, Moose
Dee, Dave Cox and the unestimable Baron Beetmoll Troy.
Mark Plunkett, Tour Manager Extraordinaire and Barry Knight, Security
with a smile and a simile. Thanx, gentlemen, for your upful vibes.
Louis Walsh - fair play to ye man - and John Reynolds, Boyzone's
management. And Carol Hannah too.
Stylist to Mr. B. Fallon - Mr. S. Lynch.

Ronan Keating, Stephen Gately, Shane Lynch, Keith Duffy and Mikey
Graham - El(vis) Mucho Thanx Y'All.
You.
Me.
Serendipity.
"Bless us who are still alive and
bless us who are still in heaven".
BP November 6th 1997.